21 Salute

Selected poems on
hope, grief & introspection

Joyeeta Sen Bose

BookLeaf
Publishing

India | USA | UK

Presentation by *BookLeaf Publishing*

Web: www.bookleafpub.com

E-mail: info@bookleafpub.com

ISBN: 9789363300491

First edition 2024

To my angels who have crossed the rainbow bridge, leaving behind a constellation of memories. To my mother, the guiding star who nurtured my growth and allowed me to explore every possible hue of life - bright, dull and vivid. To my best friend forever, Mou, who held my world in a loving embrace and shared the depths of our souls. And to my beloved husband, Raj, whose unwavering love has shaped me into who I am today in our 21 years of union. This book is a tribute to all of you, and a testament to the enduring power of human connections.

PREFACE

A Note to the Reader

In the grand tapestry of human existence, we weave stories of love, loss, triumph, and despair. These threads, often hidden from view, intertwine to create a unique narrative for each of us. "21 Salute" is an invitation to explore a corner of this vast tapestry, a glimpse into the author's personal journey.

Inspired by the naval tradition of the 21-gun salute, a symbol of the highest honor, these poems offer a tribute to the complexities of life. They delve into the depths of emotions, exploring the joys of love, the sting of loss, the resilience of the human spirit, and the power of words to connect us on a profound level.

Each poem is a reflection of the author's experiences, a testament to the beauty and fragility of life itself. May these words resonate with you, sparking your own reflections and perhaps even inspiring you to share your own stories.

Thank you for joining me on this journey.

With gratitude,

Joyeeta Sen Bose

ACKNOWLEDGEMENT

I would like to express my sincere gratitude to the following individuals and institutions for their invaluable contributions to the publication of "21 Salute":

- **Arushi,** my publishing manager from **BookLeaf Publishing,** for the unwavering support and belief in this project.

- **Ritika Dubey** for her meticulous attention to detail and expert guidance.

- **Tahira** for creating a beautiful and evocative cover that captures the essence of the book.

- **My daughter, Ritwika and son, Raunak** for their constant encouragement, love, and support throughout this journey.

- **Juno, my beautiful 2-year-old Shihtzu puppy** who has accompanied my nightly writing sessions and inspired me to be faithful to my emotions and creativity.

Finally, I would like to thank all the readers who have supported my work and shared their insights with me. Your enthusiasm and appreciation mean the world.

Contents

Epigraph - A journey of self-discovery, from doubt to delight of a girl turning 21. The metamorphosis of a teenage girl into a confident woman.

21

Where do I begin?
My teenage years have passed, yet doubts
still cling.
In the mirror I catch my reflection, I gasp and
squirm.
Oh, where are my curves, why am I so slim!

I wonder if I'll ever be a cherished, radiant
lady!
Being slender felt like a curse and went
against my body.

I was a cheerful friend to girls and boys and
peers,
But never their muse, not the one their heart
admires.

Books and research were my refuge, my
solace,
Where I didn't have to mask my empty space.
My grades soared while my friends formed
pairs to drive,
And in my prayers, I hoped for my partner to
arrive.

Days, they finally turned into a beautiful sight,
As from a cocoon, a new me emerged, bright!
Still slender and gawky but glowing with light,
With hues and charm that gave me delight.

When like magic, my special day arrived,
Blessed with two admirers, my heart rejoiced.
One love I set free, the other I held tight,
Amidst the bittersweet joy, *I turned 21
tonight!*

Epigraph - A soldier goes to fight at eighteen and dies in war. And yet the legal age for drinking is 21, the age of majority, when one has complete legal control over decisions and actions. The irony of a soldier's age makes them both heroic and a victim of societal norms.

Coming of Age

This is a tale of stars and seas.
Of deserted cities and marching beats.
At eighteen summers, fresh and green,
He got drafted to fight enemies, unseen.

With the weight of the war on fragile hands
Biting the dust of foreign lands
He trudged away from his dear home and kin
With a heavy heart and thoughts within.

He trudged away, yet hopes remain
For peace to wash away their pain,
To reunite with those they miss,
To feel again, their gentle kiss.

The battle's roar. Screams pierce the
thundered sky!
Slippery black rain muffles the soldier's cry.
And there beneath a foreign starlit horizon,
His comrades fall and sink to sleep in oblivion.

At eighteen summers, he's learned to see,
The cost of war, the silent plea.
At eighteen summers, he's grown too fast,
Through moments slipping, shadows cast.

And though the price is steep and high,
For his country and honor, he must try.
He bears the scars, reflects on pain,
How deep the loss, for the fleeting gain.

Yet back at home, the law is clear,
No drink shall pass his lips, no beer,
For he's too young, they firmly state,
To toast his friends or celebrate!

At eighteen, he's a warrior bold,
With stories of the battles told,
But twenty-one's the age decreed,
For sipping whiskey, wine or mead.

So he tips his helmet, shrugs his gun
Cocks and dips to trot-and-run,
But alas! With the bullet in his stomach
caught,
It's time he joins his comrades who fought!

Sinking into the dust, he wearily thinks,
Through tears and prayers, the true soldier
sinks.
With dreams of days when wars will cease,
And toasts to freedom, love, and peace!

This is a tale of stars and seas.
A boy of eighteen at war, who may sooner
cease!
Denied till twenty-one to raise a glass in toast!
But sacrificed his all, when he wanted to live
the most!

Epigraph - **21** grams is the physical weight of the soul, according to physician Duncan MacDougal. He calculated this by measuring the body weight before and after death, noting a loss of about 21 grams attributed to the soul leaving the body. However, Modern science hasn't supported this idea, and the concept of measuring the soul's weight remains more philosophical.

Weight of your Soul

Did you ever wonder what is the weight of your soul?
Is it light as a feather or heavy as the Roman scroll?
Does it drift in the breeze like a joyful leaf?
Or sink with the burdens of hopeless grief?

In the early century's twilight glow,
Duncan MacDougall dared to know.
He measured the weight of those who'd
passed,
In a quest for truth, his shadows cast.

"Twenty-one grams," the numbers told,
A whisper of the soul, an attempt quite bold.
Yet flaws and doubts in his method were
raised,
Left shadows in this mystic chase!

I, for one, swing betwixt this theory banned,
As science now finds no trace in this shifting
sand.
For souls elude the scales we wield,
In thoughts and dreams, their truth is
revealed.

But I am sure it weighs more than your weight
in gold,
The weight of your life story, of dreams
untold.
It's in your laughter, the tears you've shed,
The words you've spoken, the lines you've
read.

It's in the love you give and take,
The promises that you don't break.
The kindness shown to strangers and friends,
The way you lived, your means and the ends.

The weight of your soul is in your song,
The melodies that linger wide and long.
The hopes you cherish, the fears you fight,
The silent prayers you say at night.

It's in the scars that mark your heart,
The strength to rise again, and play your part.
In moments lost and those you seize,
The whispered prayers for your babies.

The weight of your soul is in the light,
The way you shine in the darkest night.
The dreams you chase, the goals you set,
The love you give without regret.

It's in your journey, not the end,
It's in your melodies that heal and mend.
The weight of your soul is vast, profound,
In every heartbeat, every sound.

So let your soul be bold and free,
Trust its journey, your soul's decree.
In the harmony of love and grace,
The music of your soul's embrace.

And cherish it, this precious weight,
In every dawn, and night so late.
For in your soul, the truth is clear,
The essence of all you hold so dear.

Epigraph - The issue of the Twenty-One Demands, which Japan proposed to China in 1915, is known to be a turning point in Japanese diplomatic history. The author here creates her own list of 21 demands from the divine which can help us through the travails of life.

21 Demands

A list of demands, from the Divine I make,
As I lie on my bed of trials, awake.
I ask for wisdom, pure and true,
As I prepare my manifesto with a clear view.

i.   Grant me patience, steady and strong,
ii.   To endure the days that feel so long.

iii.   And courage fierce to face my fears,
iv.   To stand my ground through all the
           tears.

v.   I seek your compassion, deep and
           wide,
vi.   To hold my hand and be my guide.
vii.   Send me empathy to feel others' pain,
viii.   And joyous celebrations in neighbor's
           gain.

ix.   Bestow upon me kindness bright,
x.   To spread to others day and night.
xi.   Kindness to self, first I must recognize,
xii.   That's a blessing hidden in disguise.

xiii.   Grant me strength, both body and
           soul,
xiv.   To overcome fatigue and reach my
           goal.
xv.   And clarity of vision, to find my way,
xvi.   Through the doubtful shadows of
           each long day.
xvii.   I ask for peace, serene and calm,
xviii.   To end my day with a soothing balm.
xix.   And love, to treasure pure and true,

xx.   To bind my heart, in all I do.
xxi.   Dear divine, forgiveness I seek,
           For self and others, all bold and meek.

A list of demands, neither heavy nor light,
I whisper softly into the inky night.
On my bed of blessings still, I lay,
As I dream of a bigger, brighter day.

Epigraph - In Tarot, the number 21 is related to the card The World. One of the many meanings of this card is to have the world at your feet! It may certainly feel that at the age of 21 life holds vast promises.

World at Your Feet

At 21, you have the world at your feet,
Start of a journey where dreams and reality meet.
A canvas fresh, splashed with vibrant hues,
An open road, the destination you choose.

At 21, your world is vast,
With time to learn from your present and
past.
Do seize each moment, make it last…
While you chase your dreams and run
steadfast.

With every step, new horizons unfold,
In the story of your life, adventures bold.
The promise of elixir, the thrill of the new,
Opportunities galore, framed in skies so blue.

Embrace the chances, let your spirit soar,
Explore the unknown, seek out some more.
At 21, the future is bright,
Filled with promises and boundless light.

The future shines, a beacon bright,
Promising you endless joy and delight.
The world awaits with bated breath,
For your steady step, your quest of faith.

The world at your feet, a grand romance,
A chance to sing, to love, to dance.
To forge your path, to make your stand,
With heart and soul, and a spirit grand.

At 21, embrace the thrill,
Of awakened pleasures and dreams fulfilled.
With endless paths to wander and explore,
New horizons that open new doors.

At 21, you're sprinkled with pixie dust sweet,
A tapestry of dreams, life is a treat.
With every treble, bass and beat,
Behold, the world is truly at your feet.

Epigraph - According to the Bible, there were "21 acts of rebellion" committed by the Israelites to break free from Egyptian control. It suggests a series of bold or defiant actions, each challenging norms or expectations in some way. Here's a conceptual breakdown of what these acts might be, that can serve as powerful ways to challenge the status quo and advocate for change in society.

21 Acts of Rebellion

Speak out where silent voices tend to rust,
In shadows cast by laws unjust.
Speak out against the chains that bind,
Those policies that crush spirit and mind.

Stand Up, when injustice is crushed in
deafening roars,
And breaks free from bolted doors.
The power lies in voices clear,
To shatter fear and draw us near.

Protest, unveil the masks of those in power,
Expose the deceit lurking every hour.
For justice thrives where hearts ignite,
And rallies born of shared insight.

Create Art, in public squares and hallowed
halls,
On city streets and rickety chawls.
Let your creation be strong and provoke,
To break the silence, wrath invoke.

Reject the unethical path, fraught with trials
fierce,
Yet *stand your ground* and face your fears.
For every call that dares to boycott,
Lights the way to a greater plot.

Write, speak boldly, face the storm,
With your pen as armor, justice sworn.
Fearless words, a clarinet for reform.
Courage ignites new paths to be born.

Volunteer, for in the act of serving well,
You forge the path to change for all.
Serve those wretched who lost their will,
A beacon for hopes to glow up still.

Educate, with words that cut through thick
disguise,
To *challenge* wrongs and seek the wise.
Stand tall with knowledge, let courage rise,
And pierce the dark with open eyes.

Innovate, to develop anew is to break the
mold,
To craft new paths, to be brave and bold.
In the corridors where old solutions fade,
Forge new ways with tools unafraid.

Advocate, for in the heart of every problem, a
challenge awaits,
Where shadows loom and doubt creates.
There lies a spark, a chance to see,
A *vision* born of what could better be.

Challenge Norms, see beyond the limits set,
In every trial, a chance to bet.
On novel ways to heal and mend,
To *start anew,* to make amends

Speak the Truth, where gaps are wide and
needs are deep,
Find honesty and let the lies sleep,
With reality as your guide,
Passionate fire burns bright inside.

Promote Alternatives, breathe new life into
tired schemes,
Transform the old with fresh new dreams.
From fractured hopes and scattered plans,
Build bridges strong with able hands.

Engage, go take the reins, and boldly steer,
Through challenges, both far and near.
For in the heart of every quest you meet,
Influence changes; a blessed treat.

Practice Sustainability, turn that faucet, a
mindful twist,
Save the drops that would be missed.
Recycle, sort, and waste reduce,
In every action, let purpose deduce.

Form Alliances, in a world where echoes softly call,
To heed the Earth's delicate, mysterious trail.
We *find* our way in choices made,
To *live* in harmony and not invade.

Fundraise, promote the message, loud and clear,
Let the vision of a future steer.
With every coin, with every rupee,
Together, we shape a legacy.

Question Authority, in every moment, let actions guide,
To *honor* the world, let the spirit abide.
Challenge the norms that bind the hand,
Seek the truths hidden beneath the sand.

Leverage Social Media, in the digital world,
create content that lights the way,
With vivid words and images that sway.
To raise awareness, to spark the flame,
And *mobilize others* in the quest for change.

Engage in Civil Disobedience, in peaceful
protest, let voices rise,
Against the wrongs that shadows disguise.
With hearts resolved and spirits free,
Defy the unjust, with dignity.

Celebrate Diversity, in the mosaic of our
world, so vast and bright,
Celebrate diversity, embrace the light.
In every shade, in every hue,
Find the beauty in their diverse view.

These acts can serve in powerful ways, so
challenge, advocate, and always face,
Through each act of courage and grace, we
shape our future, a better place!

Epigraph - In the realm of numerology, the number 21 is associated with creativity, independence, and personal growth. In this poem, the author encapsulates a lifetime of love—a journey of 21 years shared through sunshine and storms. Though the journey was cut short, the memories created will forever be cherished...

21 Trips Together

21 trips, around the sun, was our loving
journey together,
Each season with its passing charm, marked
our time with wonder.

From our twenty-first spring through
autumn's glow, we braved all kinds of
weather,
Bound by love, we've grown and thrived, our
souls twining forever.

This journey's been a winding road,
With kindred memories that our love
bestowed.
Blessed with children in our early years,
Our lives grew richer, our nest nurtured with
care.

Seasons change, and tides they turn,
As Mother Nature spares no one.
Relentless sun then parched our garden,
Raiding our home, threatening the youngest
one!

Shaken together, in dark turmoil,
We rose in terror, falling in prayer.
Through trials that we could barely foil,
We summoned our strength to reclaim our
heir.

This fight then took its greedy toll,
As shadows darkened and malaise took hold.
Death at my foothold most firmly stood,
Yet we fought on, as we knew we could.

Amen, a miracle blessed our lives,
As joy returned and our hearts revived.
From trials faced to dreams achieved,
In newfound grace, we all believed.

But lest we flaunt our power to exist,
Fate, she planned a cruel blow too swift.
In one crushing blow, your breath cut short,
Blowing out the light of our fort!

Alas, we never did get to see,
What you would look like, at forty and three.
The dreams we had, forever stilled,
Our trip thus ends, our journey unfulfilled.

21 trips around the sun, marked our special
journey together,
It ain't too short when I count the smiles and
a million joys of treasure.
Bound by love, we rise and grow, twin souls
that die but never,
In our heirs, we see a little bit of you and me,
our twinning souls forever.

Epigraph - What conspires in the moments before the soul struggles to decide to move on? Does the attachment to life and its many wonders hold it back or does the eternal knowledge of life and death clear the path for the soul to move on to yet another beautiful experience? This poem captures the short dilemma between life and death during a soul's transition. This is based on the actual tragic loss of her husband.

21 Minutes to Live

I was hurrying for my morning drive; I saw the clock as it struck four,
While my folks stirred in their sleep, I was already out of the door.

Through the misty light of early dawn, my car
rushed in hurried race,
Until it dashed into the mammoth truck, that
stopped abruptly in its pace.

In the first minute: an eerie, deafening crash
put me in shock,
Heart raced, confusion reigned, my body
arched in a deathlock.
The second minute: breath grew tight, my
eyes split open, filled with fright,
A blaze of memories terrorized my mind, as I
fought with might for my failing sight.

Third minute: a searing pain, soundless
screams as blood chokes me deep,
Mind wrestles in disbelief as I lay buried in
steel, begging for merciful eternal sleep.
By the fourth: my senses dim, the body
weakens, thoughts grow grim,
A wisp of names, a final plea, for those who'll
grieve - parents, kids, wife and kin.

In the fifth minute, acceptance nears, a flood
of thoughts, desperate prayers,

My mangled body beyond repair, a pitiful
sight, my soul prepares.
From the edge of life into the light, the
minutes tick loud, from sixth to tenth,
Faces of beloved a clear array, moments of
joy, of strife, of fleeting strength.

By the eleventh, a calm descends, the grip of
fear, it slowly ends,
A sense of peace, a strange embrace, as time
slips by in a tender bend.
From twelfth to fifteenth, whispers soft,
voices so loving, gently hailed,
At the sixteenth minute a final breath, taken
deep but never exhaled.

An end to pain, an end to fear, in the
seventeenth my soul ascends,
Eighteenth to twentieth, a silent salute to
realms unknown, that wise commends.
A final look upon my body I gaze, twisted and
trapped in a deathly maze.
The final chapter gently closes, when at the
twenty-first minute, my spirit rises.

In calm I watch the flutter beneath; of sirens,
screams, of running feet,
In vain they try for me to revive, the broken
fabric of a fleeting life.
I watch my family dissolve in plight, I yearn to
tell darling, it will be alright.
As I step from earth to beyond, I know I will
remain in their future bright.

A life remembered, held so dear,
The soul transcends, knowing no fear.
I am not the body, not even the mind.
My final lesson, as I leave the world behind.

Epigraph - For soulmates, the angel number 21 can be a positive sign and a reminder to trust in the spiritual essence of love. By trusting the path, one can experience deeper connection even after life ends. This poem is an ode to life itself, which continues even after a tragedy.

Beyond 21 years of love

The house has gone quiet, where laughter
once rang,
Echoes of fights, snuggles, romance, now
softly hang.
The sink in the sofa, an empty left-side of the
bed,
A couple's warm presence has gently fled.

21 years of sweat, joy and pain,
Of busy mornings and evening rain.
Growing up together through thrift and
strong,
Never prepared for a solo dance so long.

Each corner holds a piece of the man,
In every dream shared, now undone.
As the kids reflect his smiling eyes,
Alone she treads, with silent sighs.

Strangely, the world spins and moves apace,
How strange is that, when she seeks his grace.
In photographs, letters, cards of old,
Freezing their story, two hearts do hold.

Friends come by with kind intent,
But seldom they bring true heart's content.
Yet in the stillness, she finds his guiding light,
Shining his wisdom through the darkest night.

The life they had, the bond they shared,
Still blooms in silence, their souls still paired.
In every tear, in every smile,
Love sustains, their promises on aisle.

She carries on, as he would wish,
Shouldering the load of home, hearth and
their kids.
For in the afterlife, she knows there remains,
A chance to share the fruits of her pains.

21 years, a chapter closed,
Yet beyond them, lives composed.
A solitary woman moves forward through
strife,
Forever embraced by the love of her life.

Epigraph - On July 21, "National Be Someone Day" challenges each of us to take ten seconds to make a meaningful difference in a child's life.

Make A Difference

Aah the innocence of kids, a precious gem,
Trust and joy, the beauty that adorns them.
Through the eyes of a child, the world must
be seen,
A canvas of wonder, pure and pristine.

Yet, the kids today, in shadows they stand,
Tiny fingers reaching up, seeking a guiding
hand.
For youths and adults alike in their pursuit,
Buried in a digital world, deaf and mute.

Immersed are the kids in their forlorn land,
When adults have stopped to lend a child
their hand.
Forgotten that their role is to shape, to guide,
to stand.
Words of kindness, to kids, their magic wand.

Eyes once bright now dim with despair,
Children left on their own, with no one to
care.
On lonely beds, their tears are shed,
Muffled cries in the night that go unsaid.

Adults and Youth! You can plant dreams in
kids anew,
In tender hearts, flickering the hopes of few.
Each moment spent, each lesson shared,
Leaves a lasting imprint on kids, showing you
cared.

Through laughter and tears, through ups and
downs,
In a kid's story, your presence forever crowns.
A beacon of light in the darkest night,
For a kid, you are a source of strength, a
guiding light.

To inspire a child's mind, to ignite their soul,
To help them reach their highest goal.
Hey adult, with your acts of love and care,
You can make a difference, be a treasure rare.

Every child, whether rich or poor,
Needs to know how much we care.
They search for love that's never there,
A burden too heavy for them to bear.

To believe in them, to see a child through,
Is to change the world, and make it a better
place true!

Epigraph - Number 21 combines the energy of 2 and the balance and partnership represented by 1. It symbolizes the beginning of a new stage or chapter in life, but with balance and teamwork.

Power of 2 and 1

Clever math scientists, a saga they told
About "2" and "1" and the secrets they hold.

Each with a power, a story to tell,
A numerological spell they weave so well.

1, stands alone, shining a beacon bright,
A symbol of leadership, of purest light.

1, the pioneer, the path it paves,
With courage bold, sails unknown waves.

1, speaks of beginnings, a fresh new start,
A single step with a lion's heart.

In the realm of thoughts, "1" stands supreme,
The essence of self, the spark of a dream.

Then comes 2, with a softer grace,
A number that holds intuition, in loving
embrace.

2, brings balance; it's harmony's call,
It attracts unity, finds true strength for all.

2 is the call for pair, the bond so true,
Reflective partners, attracting me and you.

2 is the essence of the duality's dance,
The quality when opposites exist, in authentic
chance.

While 1 represents sun, in solitary blaze,
2 represents moon, queen of terrific sixth
sense.

Together they weave interesting fabrics of life,
With balance and empathy, when they
express, they thrive.

1 initiates the path it clears,
2 collaborates, soothing the fears.

In numerology, 21's dance is divine,
A cosmic rhythm, a powerful sign.

Mathematics property of Number 21 is the
first Blum integer,
As it's a semiprime, both its prime factors
being Gaussian prime number.

Heed the wisdom number 21 impart,
Of independence, growth, and a unified
heart.

Together they carry positive vibrations,
Of balanced power, expanded horizons.

Epigraph - Often tiny tales are complete marvels in themselves. Set to poems, they bring out the best.

A Dozen Tiny Tales

1.   **The Lost Key**
        Frantically, she searched everywhere,
        tearing her room apart.
        Sinking in relief, she found the key
        stuck between the pages of a book.
        She'd used it as a bookmark.

2.   **The Secret Note**
        A child found an old note tucked in a
        library book.

A decades-old message from a past
reader read:
"Not everyone will read paperbacks
anymore. Technology will eventually
kill this fantasy world" it said.

3.   **The Stray Dog**
He fed a stray dog every day through
winter, sharing a portion of his own
warm dinner. One night, when he was
bitter and sad, the dog brought him a
lost wallet. Inside, he found his own
ID. It was Thanksgiving.

4.   **The Forgotten**
One last check of her attic, and she
stumbled upon a dusty teddy bear.
In her hands, memories came flooding
back; bedtime stories, whispered
secrets, comforting kisses and hugs.
"Coming!" she called out to the
impatient voice. Her son was taking
her on a new journey: Peaceful Pines
Elder Care.

5.   **That Rainy Day**
Stuck in crazy traffic, her frustration
began to melt when she noticed the
elderly couple in the car ahead.
Two grey heads leaned together, one
hand clasping the other's shoulder.
The windshield sticker read, "Please
be Patient. Disability is Diverse."

6.   **The Old Tree**
The children carved their names into
the old tree.
Years later, they returned. Now
elderly, for a school reunion, finding
their initials still carved into the bark.
Time preserved their youthful promise
of eternity. The tree now basked in
autumn mirth.

7.   **The Café Encounter**
Two strangers shared a table at a
crowded café.
They discovered they had the same
birthday. They shared a cake and a
candle.
Today is another birthday, and now
they share their lives.

8. **The Missed Call**
    She had missed his call, a long time
    back. Later, at her best friend's
    wedding, she found an old voicemail
    he had left then. He had proposed to
    her.

9. **For the ones who Grew up Early**
    The ones who dealt with the loss of a
    parent at an early age, you were just a
    child. You had to quickly grow up, to
    step into big boots.
    Protect yourselves. Play normal. Don't
    play invisible, to not come up as
    needy.
    You deserve to let go, to fail. To feel
    safe without fighting for it all.

10. **The Birthday Wish**
    She blew out her birthday candles
    alone, wishing for love. The doorbell
    rang, and there stood her childhood
    sweetheart. "Dad! You remembered!"

11. **The Gardener**
    An elderly woman's garden thrived
    under her tender care. She spoke
    gently to each plant, nurturing them

with kind words. The garden thrived
with vibrant fruits and flourishing
blooms. The only sound she could
hear was their whispered gratitude.

12. The Letter

A letter arrived in the mail, decades
late. It was from a soldier, informing
his family he was finally coming home.
The elderly widow quietly put on the
kettle. It was time to welcome him, at
last.

Epigraph - Key pendants are customarily given as a gift on the 21st birthday, when you are considered old enough to be a key-holder to your family's home, and thus hold a symbolical 'senior' position in the family. Can a gift for 21st birthday be the key to heart?

A Key to Pure Love

For my 21st, dawned a special day,
A new friend arrived, in a funny way.
With eyes luminous, bright and big,
Licked me a pup, tiny as a guinea pig.

With baby paws, she snuggled my heart,
A darting pink tongue, made licking an art.
Promptly, hopelessly I loved her to tears,
My snow-white girl with jet-black ears.

The furry bundle, with wobbly steps,
Followed me around, with her sniffs and
pecks.
My heart swelled with fierce, protective
affection,
As we surrendered fully to our divine
connection.

I watched her grow up, a beautiful young pup,
As slowly she learnt to eat, drink, fetch and
jump.
With every step, a beautiful bond we weaved,
A tireless wagging tail, in trust and love
believed.

At night, her warmth, curled at my feet lay,
Even in her dreams, her loyalty would convey:
A friend for life, my guardian dear,
In your presence, there's nothing to fear.

Morning goodbyes were a forlorn affair,
Drowning my heart with her desolate stare.
Evenings were filled with excitement true,
As she danced delighted, kicking a hullabaloo.

My 21st marked a wondrous start,
Juno, my fur-baby, awakened my nurturing
heart.
Here's to us, to our best years ahead,
Hope you live longest, with countless
memories made.

A dog's friendship is the purest bliss,
Sealed with trust and a warm, wet kiss.

Epigraph - What is the significance of the number 21 in religions? 21 is considered the number of perfections, it is the number of the Holy Scriptures, it is the number of times the mantra Om is chanted during Aumkara, the ancient Hindu practice.

21 Tales of Wisdom

In ancient scrolls and stories old,
Lives 21 tales, of wisdom bold.
From sages wise and seers of jiu-jitsu,
Lessons planned, for me and you.

The first speaks of patience, calm and still,
Like a river's journey, past a hill.
The second whispers of courage bright,
A warrior's heart in the darkest night.

The third tale weaves a fabric of trust,
In bonds unbroken, strong and just.
The fourth praises the power of love,
A gift from earth, and heavens above.

The fifth talks of kindness, simple and pure,
A tender heart and giving hand for sure.
The sixth harps about the virtue of grace,
In every step and every place.

The seventh tale reveals the story of light,
In seeking truth, our guiding sight.
Eighth speaks of balance, to harmonize our
way,
To find the mid-path day after day.

The ninth tale honors, wisdom pursued,
In seeking knowledge, we truly are blessed.
The tenth sings praises of forgiveness sweet,
A soul unburdened is a heart complete.

The eleventh tale is of strength within,
In facing our fears, we rise, we win.
The twelfth exalts the power of our dreams,
In visions high, life's spirit beams.

The thirteenth whispers, of faith and trust,
In divine forces, believe we must.
Fourteenth tale is of a joyful face,
In every smile, a blessed grace.

The fifteenth speaks, of peace profound,
In a silent mind, and in acceptance found.
Sixteenth tells that hope is a bright flame,
Burning in hearts to reach our aim.

The seventeenth credits the gift of time,
Every minute spent, a moment sublime.
Eighteenth tale is about nature's role,
Every fruit and leaf, our universe whole.

The nineteenth extols heavy, on unity,
Together we stand, a powerful community.
The twentieth tale is of life's flow,
After every end, a new start does follow.

And twenty-first, the final tale,
Life's a great journey, just follow the trail.
In wisdom's light, our paths shine bright,
21 tales, a gift divine.

Epigraph - What is the significance of sacrifice in the name of God? A reflection on the true nature of offerings and the path to divine connection. Beyond material sacrifices, true devotion lies in purifying the soul and embracing the divinity within.

Offerings Supreme

The first offering was made by Cain, Adam's first, to God.
It was his farm's best produce, to thank his dear merciful Lord.
Abel offered the firstborn of his flock.
That God accepted, along with pieces of fat block.

When Moses led, the Israelites gave their
one-tenth or tithe,
For the land they were promised and wars till
date, the fight.

I believe offerings never worked like the
pagans imagined.
It's as if you're trading things with God to
have your wishes fulfilled.
No, my friend, sacrifices do not work or
please the Divine anymore.
He does not delight in the blood of bulls or
lambs, of goats or bores.

Says the Lord, "Wash yourselves, make
yourselves clean;
Remove the evil of your deeds, search for me
within.
Cease to do evil, correct oppression, learn to
do good.
Bring justice to the fatherless, end the plague
of widowhood."

Daily offerings of food, water, incense, gold,
silk, and milk.
While zillions go naked and hungry - minions
in their ilk!
"What to me is the multitude of your
sacrifice?"
Speaks the Lord, "Bring no more vain
offerings, burden to my eyes."

Thus, would speak the Brahman, the eternal
conscious, the infinite.
Atman - your soul, is a part of me within,
knows your wrong from right.
When you reside the divinity within,
What use are material offerings to me?

Rid yourself of the debts, while enjoying in my
image reborn.
Repay the generosity of your parents and
ancestors you adorn.
Bow to ancient sages, to knowledge passed
down,
It is their guidance that gives us success,
peace, and prosperity abound.

Be grateful to the society that shapes your
identity,
And to humanity, your shared community.
Show gratitude to Mother Earth, who
generously provides,
Abundant fruits, leaves, roots, and water that
freely abides.

To the divine Supreme energies: air, water,
earth, fire, and space,
Bow and offer your sublime ablutions in
abundant grace.

Epigraph - The 21st day of the third month, known as World Down Syndrome Day, raises awareness and promotes inclusivity for individuals with Down syndrome. The choice of the date, with its 21st day, symbolizes the presence of an extra copy of the 21st chromosome that causes Down syndrome. It serves as a reminder of the importance of acceptance, support, and understanding for individuals with Down syndrome and their families.

An Ode to the 21st Day of the Third Month

Every 21st day of the third month, we gather,
A date chosen to symbolize our quirky fate
rather.
To reflect on the journey, the path that's
embraced,
Of those with an extra chromosome, bravely
graced.

The 21st day stands for the 21st gene,
A tiny difference, touching babies serene.
In the fabric of life, it weaves a challenging
thread,
Sagas of unshakeable love, guiding parents
ahead.

For in that extra chromosome, there's a world
to behold,
A narrative of courage, that's beautifully told.
To support and to understand, with hearts
open wide,
To walk in honor with these families, like
soldiers by our side.

Acceptance is key, in a world that's diverse,
To cherish each moment, for better or worse.
To uplift and to honor, the strength that's
within,
To embrace every triumph, let the celebration
begin.

On this special day, the power of 21st we hold
dear,
We pledge our support, our patience, and our
cheer.
For individuals with Down Syndrome and their
special kin,
We humbly stand together, saluting their
strength within.

The choice of this date is a reminder so clear,
Of the beauty in difference, the message we
share.
Every person is valued, each story unique,
In the tapestry of life, it's understanding we
seek.

Let's honor the courage, the dreams that
ignite,
The spirit that soars, towards the distant light.

For, in every big challenge, when a triumph is
found,
In every heart hope surges, possibilities
abound.

In each unique soul's journey, a story unfolds,
A tale of strength and valor, that sacredly
holds.
Here's to the joy, the laughter, the tears,
To the journey of life, through all of their
years.

Let's honor this day with compassion and
care,
A salute to the families, their stories to share.
On the 21st day of the third month, we honor
and say,
World Down Syndrome Day, let's light the
way.

Epigraph - During a hypnosis session, you undergo a process that helps you relax deeply and focus your mind. This state is similar to sleep, though your mind remains highly alert and is able to respond to suggestions better. While in this relaxed state, it's believed that you're more willing to focus on your subconscious mind.

21 Steps to Inner Peace

In a quiet room where shadows softly blend,
Begins your journey, a path you'll transcend.
Twenty-one steps, for mind to descend,
Unlocking the secrets, for life to mend.

Step one: the breath, a calm, gentle embrace,
Inhale deeply and find your own pace.
Step two: close your eyes with serene grace,
Let the world fade, find your sacred space.

Step three: a soothing voice, a melody clear,
Guides you softly, your doubts disappear.
Step four: imagine a gentle blue sea,
Waves of calm, setting your spirit free.

Step five: count each wave that dances in
your mind,
One by one, leave your worries behind.
Step six: let your body gently start to sway,
Feel your tension ease and drift away.

Step seven: a staircase appears sturdy and
bright,
Twenty-one steps to the depth, promises the
mighty flight.
Step eight: take your first step, steady and
slow,
Let stress dissolve, and tranquility flow.

Step nine: each step draws you deeper into trance,
With each descent, find a lighter dance.
Step ten: the world above starts to blur and retreat,
As you spiral inward, in peace complete.

Step eleven: go deeper with each stride,
Feel the mellow calmness grow inside.
Step twelve: surrender fully to this flow,
Embrace the trust that starts to grow.

Step thirteen: a place of pure stillness found,
Where the whispers of the mind warmly resound.
Step fourteen: let the images slowly arise,
From deep within, where your truth lies.

Step fifteen: trust the beautiful process, let it be,
In this abandoned state, you're truly free.
Step sixteen: the world outside gets rapidly blurred,
In this profound silence, your soul is now heard.

Step seventeen: go, explore the hidden deep,
Where memories and dreams softly tread.
Step eighteen: observe your thoughts with
tender care,
Answers to your questions will soon be there.

Step nineteen: in this ecstatic, serene retreat,
All your senses gently, rejoice and meet.
Step twenty: let tranquility within you grow,
In this peaceful space, let your inner light
show.

Step twenty-one: you've reached your core,
Where your subconscious mind has all the
cure.
In this trance, you're free to see,
The depths of your mind with clarity.

In twenty-one steps, you've travelled deep,
Into the realms where your secrets sleep.
You've unlocked your treasure, you've found
the key,
In your sacred space, your wisdom set you
free.

Unsung Tale of Two Decades

For 21 years, she walked these halls,
Her footsteps echoed in endless calls.
A woman who toiled, heart and mind,
Unsung, unseen, and pushed behind.

Through sleepless nights and endless days,
She worked to excel in every way.
Ideas new, solutions found,
Her name was but, lost aground.

Peers got lauded, promotions gained,
She stood by clapping, her spirits strained.
After pouring her heart and soul,
Her fame and credits, others stole.

Years of meetings, plans and dreams,
Lost in the corporate jungle beams.
The glass ceiling above so high,
Dimmed the lights in her starry eyes.

Countless projects, deadlines tight,
She stayed the course, through every fight.
Her efforts stolen, her name erased,
In shadows deep, her talents placed.

A hundred doubts fill her mind with dread,
She doubts her skills, her heart oft bled.
Took a toll in decades two.
Lost her will to strive for due.

For 21 years, she shone her light,
Though unseen, she did burn bright.
In every task, she left her mark,
Among her peers, a hidden spark.

In her heart raged a smoldering fire,
A burning flame of unquenched desire.
Recognition, may never come from them,
Yet she had no will to fight or to condemn.

Away she stepped from the work she loved,
Her best decades, she gave unreserved.
Now to build a legacy of her own,
With courage and grit, she grew and shone.

To women workers, brave and bold,
Whose stories remain forever untold,
May there soon come a day that's just,
When equality and inclusion become a reality
must.

So here's to her, and women alike,
Who strive to shine despite the divide.
Your worth is more than they care to praise,
Create your trophy, carve successful days!

Epigraph - 21st century: The current era is often referred to as the 21st century. It began on January 1, 2001, and will end on December 31, 2100. This poem is a tribute to an era of maximum change.

A Tribute to the 21st Century

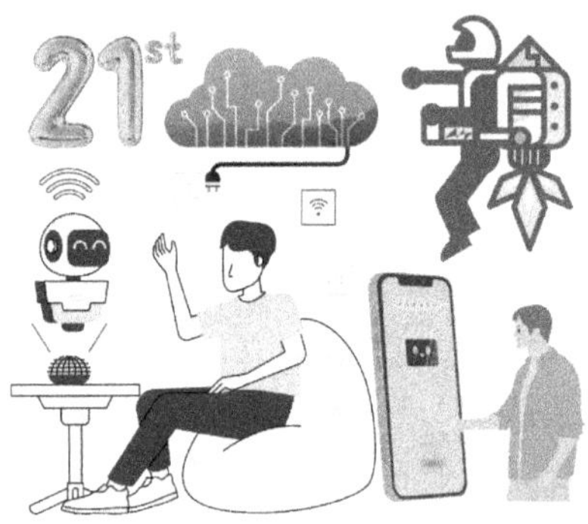

In the dawn of the 21st, a new era began,
With inventions and events in a rapid span.
It all started on January 1, 2001,
Dreams ignited by the rising sun.
And it ends on December 31, 2100, yonder,
A century's span, a journey of wonder.

The digital age unfurled its might,
With smartphones connecting us day and
night.
The Internet of Things, a vast, grand web,
Binding the world in a spidery thread.

Artificial intelligence took the central throne,
Algorithms and answers to every question
known.
Learning and thinking, evolving each day,
Reclaiming our lives in every way.

Social media rose with a powerful voice,
Giving the masses a platform of choice.
From tweets to posts, from shares to likes,
Reels traveled fast, selling ideas day and night.

Solar and Electric cars did glide,
With Tesla leading, a green tide.
Renewable energy surged in might,
Harnessing the sun, wind, and light.

Vaccines swift in a pandemic fight,
Medical marvels, our resilient light.
SpaceX rockets to the heavens soared,
Mars reached; new frontiers explored.

Quantum leaps in computing made,
With bits and qubits, new paths laid.
Unraveling mysteries of the quantum state,
Opening doors to a future great.

Climate change, a looming threat,
The stage is set, to start a re-set.
The world united to take a stand,
To heal and preserve our precious land.

But challenges rose in dark disguise,
Wars and conflicts, with religious cries.
Terror struck, and nations clashed,
Innocent lost in the violent thrash.

Economic crises shook the ground,
Financial ruins and loss profound.
Global lockdowns, put lives at stake,
Forcing humanity to bend, even break.

Social divides and justice sought,
Movements risen and battles fought.
Voices raised for rights and peace,
Squashed and stamped for strife to cease.

As decades pass and centuries wane,
The milestones of 21st remain.
A tribute to progress, and global harm,
Crafted a saga, a collective charm.
From 2001's dawn to 2100's closing song,
A century etched in history long.

Epigraph - A reflection on the unpredictable nature of life, where setbacks and triumphs intertwine. Through the metaphor of a game, this poem encourages resilience and the pursuit of goals despite the inevitable challenges.

Snake and Ladder: Life's turns

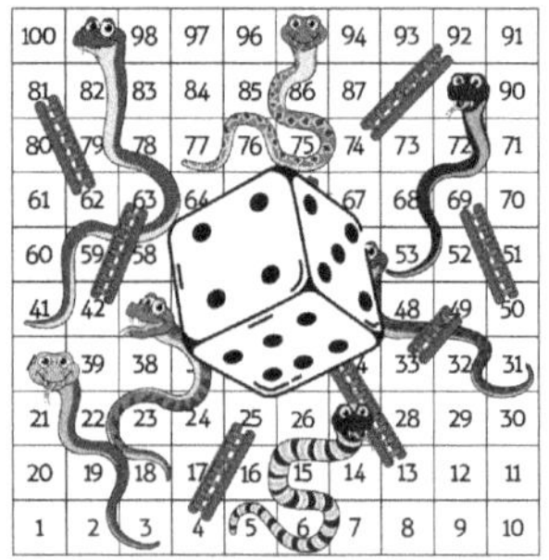

Life's a game of snake and ladder,
Where dreams can soar, then swiftly shatter.
You may climb with hope, each step
hard-earned,
But fate's sharp twists can leave you spurned.

With a roll of dice, you may near the top,
You taste excitement—sighting a successful
stop.
But lurking nearby, a snake awaits,
A sudden drop may seal shifting fates.

You climb the ladder, heart aglow,
Your efforts pay, you're in the flow.
Yet one misstep, and you lose it all—
The heights you reached, hit a sudden fall.

It's a game of risks, both high and low,
With victories sweet and bitter woe.
But those who rise, despite each sting,
Keep climbing ladders through thick and thin.

Every fall, is a chance to rise,
To shake off dust and reach the skies.
Though snakes may strike, don't yield to
fear—
The game's not over till all is clear.

So roll your dice, embrace the race,
For life's a game played with luck and grace.
Will guide your moves through joy and pain—
Up the ladder, down again.

Epigraph - Mother's love is a force both gentle and fierce, a nurturing embrace that remains constant through every season of life. It is a love that gives without asking, protects without pause, and sacrifices without regret. It speaks in whispers of comfort during sleepless nights and roars with pride at every triumph, big or small. A silent strength that goes unacknowledged.

When I Do Not Wake Up Tomorrow

When morning's kiss no longer warms my brow,
And silence greets the caws of the morning crow,

The sun will still blaze the morning sky,
As the moon and stars bid a shy goodbye.

My city will awaken with purpose anew,
Young and old rushing, with much to do.
When I do not wake up tomorrow, you see,
Nothing will stop, life bustles ceaselessly.

In my bed, I will be found still, by my furry
friend,
Craving my touch, she'd lick my cold face
again and again.
Mourn not for the woman dead, celebrate her
life instead!
A lone sailor, her ship through storms fierce,
she braved.

When I do not wake up tomorrow, my dears,
know this true,
The hands that shaped your world, wish only
joy for you.
Please forget the strict vigilance, as you flew
my nest,
But do remember the vows, the oaths and
promises I'd kept.

So, when I do not wake with tomorrow's
dawn,
Do not mourn my fading years of solitude
gone.
Remember, my love—steadfast and true,
The shoulders you stood on, that carried you
through.

I leave behind no debt, no stain;
My legacy clear for you to claim.
I bore my solitary role with pride,
Setting your desires above mine.

With thoughts and prayers, I paved the way
For you to rise better each day.
A tale of love, resilience and might:
A mother's hope, beyond your sight.

When tomorrow I soar through the crystal
blue skies,
Matching oceans rushing by,
Pride, not fear, fills my heart—
I gave my all, I did my part.

When I have to wake no more, I pray,
In clear unison my children will say,
"She did good, our mother, she tried;
She faltered plenty, but her love never died."

A Call to Reflection

As you close this collection, take a moment to let the words linger. Let them settle in the quiet corners of your mind, where your own experiences and emotions gently resonate in rhythm with these poems.

What stories do they evoke? The journey doesn't end here; it continues in your heart and mind. This is an invitation - for reflection and release - to give wings to your passion and weave magic with your words.

Someday, we will meet again - in your pages or mine. Live well!

www.ingramcontent.com/pod-product-compliance
Lightning Source LLC
La Vergne TN
LVHW050920200726
843508LV00011B/2242